PERPLEXING
PUZZLES
and TANTALIZING
TEASERS

PERPLEXING
PUZZLES
and
TANTALIZING
TEASERS

by Martin Gardner

ILLUSTRATED BY *Laszlo Kubinyi*

SIMON & SCHUSTER   *New York*

First Printing

SBN 671-65057-2 Trade
SBN 671-65058-0 Library
Library of Congress Catalog Card Number: 69-16871
Manufactured in the United States of America
Designed by Irving Perkins
Printed by The Murray Printing Co., New York
Bound by Edition Book Bindery, New Jersey

FOR MY NEPHEW
Harold Berg Gardner

CONTENTS

INTRODUCTION

This is a collection of many different kinds of puzzles, some old, some new, but most of them will (I hope) be puzzles you haven't seen or heard before. None of them is very difficult, but some of the puzzles are tricky, with answers that will surprise and amuse you.

The solution to each puzzle is given at the end of the book, but of course you won't get much fun out of this collection if you start peeking at the answers before you've done your best to solve the puzzles first.

Happy puzzling!

MARTIN GARDNER

1 *Ridiculous Riddles*

1. What is green and flies through the air?
2. What is yellow and always points north?
3. What did the five-hundred-pound mouse say to the cat?
4. What is black and white and red all over?
5. Who was the tallest President of the United States?
6. How do you make a hippopotamus float?
7. How does an elephant put his trunk in the alligator's mouth?
8. What has a hump, is brown, and lives at the North Pole?
9. What's red, then purple, then red, then purple . . . ?
10. What does *decor* mean?
11. What do you sit on, sleep on, and brush your teeth with?
12. What has 2,754 seeds and moves by itself?
13. What has 18 legs, is covered with red spots, and catches flies?

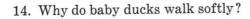

14. Why do baby ducks walk softly?

15. What is round and green, is covered with blue hair, has big scaly claws, weighs five thousand pounds, and goes peckety-peck-peck?
16. What has four stander-uppers, four puller-downers, two hookers, two lookers, and a swishy-wishy?
17. How do you top a car?
18. Why does Smokey the Bear wear a forest ranger's hat?

2   Handies

Have you ever heard of "handies"? That was the name of a popular puzzle game everybody was playing in the 1930's. The idea was to do something silly with your hands and ask "What's this?" People tried to guess. If they couldn't guess correctly, you told them what it was. For example, the first handie shown here is "Indian peeking over his indoor television antenna." Now see how good you are at guessing the others.

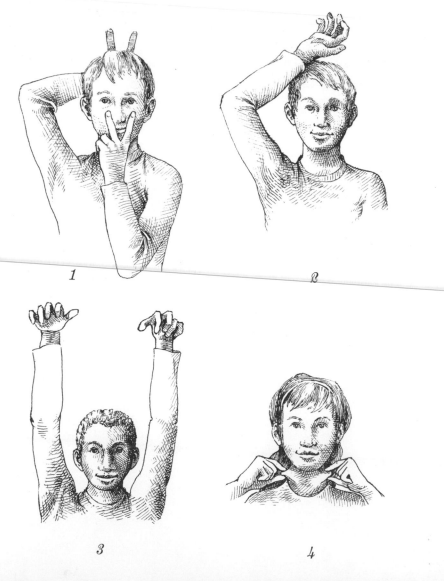

1

2

3

4

5

6

7

13

3 *Fun with Palindromes*

Palindromes are words or sentences that are the same when read backward or forward. The picture shows how Adam, when he first met Eve, might have introduced himself by speaking a palindrome, and how Eve might have replied by speaking another. Even the serpent is uttering a palindrome!

There are hundreds of longer sentences that read the same both ways. Here are a few clever ones:

STRAW? NO TOO STUPID A FAD. I PUT SOOT ON WARTS.
A MAN, A PLAN, A CANAL—PANAMA!
WAS IT A BAR OR A BAT I SAW?
DRAW PUPIL'S LIP UPWARD
TEN ANIMALS I SLAM IN A NET
POOR DAN IS IN A DROOP
NO, IT IS OPEN ON ONE POSITION

How good are you at recognizing a palindromic word when you come across one in your reading? To test yourself, see how many such words you can find in the following paragraphs:

"Look at the sun, over there behind that radar tower," said Hannah. "I think it looks much redder than it did at noon."

"Wow! It sure does, Ma'am," exclaimed Otto, bending over to pat the head of a small brown pup with black markings over one eye.

4 *The Lost Star*

A perfect five-pointed star is hidden somewhere in the pattern of this patchwork quilt. Can you find it?

5 Find the Hidden Animals

In each of the sentences below, the name of an animal is concealed. The first sentence is marked so you can see how the word "dog" is hidden.

Can you find the animal in each of the other sentences?

1. What shall I <u>do, G</u>ertrude?

2. Asking nutty questions can be most annoying.

3. A gold key is not a common key.

4. Horace tries in school to be a very good boy.

5. People who drive too fast are likely to be arrested.

6. Did I ever tell you, Bill, I once found a dollar?

7. John came late to his arithmetic class.

8. I enjoy listening to music at night.

6 *Tricky Questions*

Each puzzle on this page has a funny "catch" to it. Think hard and try to guess the joke before you peek at any of the answers.

HIGGS'S PIGS

Farmer Higgs owns three pink pigs, four brown pigs, and one black pig. How many of Higgs's pigs can say that it is the same color as another pig on Higgs's farm?

PENNIES FOR SALE

Why are 1966 pennies worth almost twenty dollars?

POP AND GRANDPOP

Tom says his grandfather is only six years older than his father. Is that possible?

THROUGH THE PIPE

Jim and Tom find a long piece of pipe in a vacant lot. It's big enough so that each boy can just manage to squeeze into it and crawl from one end to the other. If Jim and Tom go into the pipe from opposite ends, is it possible for each boy to crawl the *entire length* of the pipe and come out the other end?

18

7 The Five Airy Creatures

Jonathan Swift, who wrote *Gulliver's Travels*, also wrote this clever puzzle-poem:

> *We are little airy creatures,*
> *All of different voice and features;*
> *One of us in "glass" is set,*
> *One of us you'll find in "jet,"*
> *T'other you may see in "tin,"*
> *And the fourth a "box" within.*
> *If the fifth you should pursue,*
> *It can never fly from "you."*

Can you guess who or what the five "little airy creatures" are?

8   *The Maze of the Minotaur*

An ancient Greek myth tells how Theseus found his way through a huge labyrinth, a confusing network of passageways some of which lead only to a dead end, and killed the Minotaur —a ferocious creature, half man and half bull—who lived at the center. Here is a picture showing what the plan of the labyrinth could have been. No one has ever drawn a maze that *looks* easier to work, but actually is so difficult.

Use the point of a toothpick, so you won't mark up the page and ruin the puzzle for someone else. You'll be lucky if you can find your way to the Minotaur in less than twenty minutes!

START HERE

9 The Dime-and-Penny Switcheroo

Put two dimes and two pennies in the spaces that contain their pictures. The object is to make the pennies and dimes change places in *exactly eight moves*.

You are allowed two kinds of moves:

1. You can *slide* any coin into an empty space next to it.

2. You can *jump* any coin over the coin next to it, like a jump in checkers, provided you land on an empty space.

The puzzle isn't as easy as it looks. Time yourself to see how long it takes you to switch the coins in eight moves. If you solve it in five minutes, you're a genius. Ten minutes is excellent. Twenty minutes is about average.

Remember, only eight moves are allowed. If you do it in *more* moves, you haven't solved the puzzle.

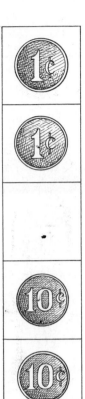

10 A Dozen Droodles for Nimble Noodles

"Droodles" are drawings made with just a few simple lines. The word was invented by Roger Price, who has written several very funny books about them. At first a droodle doesn't look like anything. But if you study it for a while, sometimes you will suddenly see what it is. Sometimes you'll *never* guess correctly. See how many of these droodles you can guess before you look at the answers.

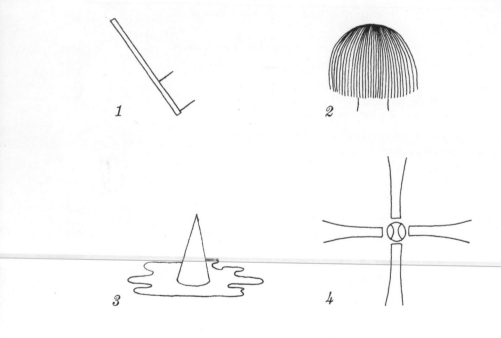

1

2

3

4

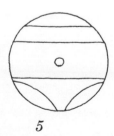

5

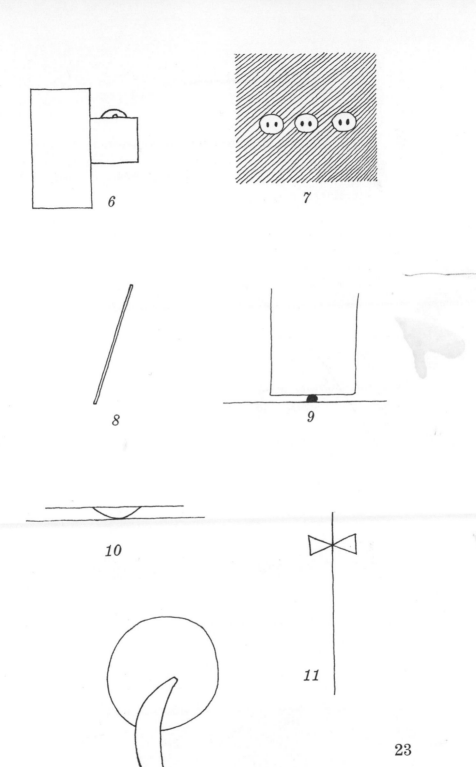

6

7

8

9

10

11

12

23

11 *Tantalizing Toothpick Teasers*

You'll need about fifteen toothpicks, or burned wooden matches, to test your wits on these six clever toothpick puzzles. If you can solve three, you're average. Four is good, five is excellent, and six makes you a genius.

1. Change the positions of four toothpicks to make three small squares, all the same size, and no toothpicks left over.
2. Change the positions of two toothpicks to make four small squares, all the same size, and no toothpicks left over.
3. Remove six toothpicks completely, leaving ten on the table.
4. Move the position of one toothpick and make the house face east instead of west.
5. Change the positions of three toothpicks so that the triangular pattern points down instead of up.
6. The picture shows how to make four triangles with nine toothpicks. Can you find a way to make four triangles, all the same size as the ones shown, with only six toothpicks?

Hint: The solution to this toothpick teaser is different from the other five. It will require a completely new approach.

1

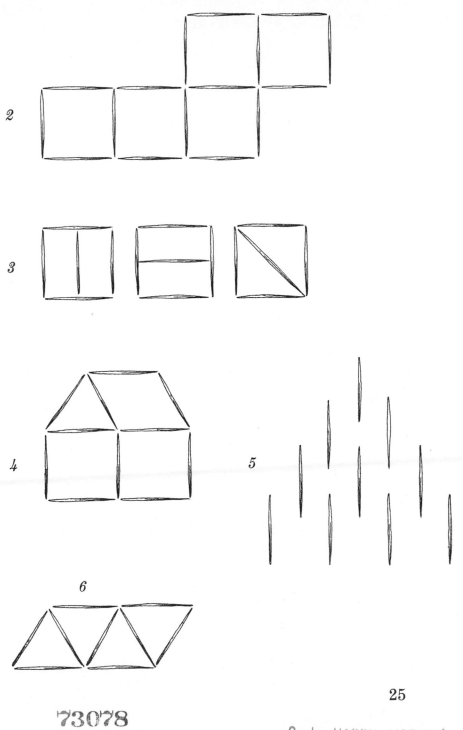

2

3

4

5

6

12 *Read the Thriftigrams*

The more words you use in a telegram, the more it costs, so you can save money if you can think of clever ways to cut down the number of words and still say everything you want to say. The thriftigram is a telegram that does this by using many single words that are puns for several words. For example, instead of saying, "Thank you very much," you can say, "Sanctuary much," and have only two words instead of four.

Now see if you can read correctly the three thriftigrams shown here.

1

DOMESTIC		**EASTERN UNION**		INTERNATIONAL	
Check Service Desired				Check Service Desired	
THRIFTIGRAM		**THRIFTIGRAM**		FULL RATE	
DAY LETTER				LETTER	
NIGHT LETTER				SHORE-SHIP	

NO. WDS.	PD. OR COLL.	NO.	CHARGE TO	TIME

To_____ Date_____
Address_____
City_____ State_____

MESSAGE:

OMNIVOROUS HAPPY SIAM
VENOM WITH YOU. LOVE
ENCASES.

2

EASTERN UNION
THRIFTIGRAM

NO. WDS.	PD. OR COLL.	NO.	CHARGE TO	TIME

To_____ Date_____

Address_____

City_____ State_____

MESSAGE:

HAVE TOOTHACHE PLANE.

CANOE MIMI AT AIRPORT?

3

EASTERN UNION
THRIFTIGRAM

NO. WDS.	PD. OR COLL.	NO.	CHARGE TO	TIME

To_____ Date_____

Address_____

City_____ State_____

MESSAGE:

VALUE BEMOAN VALENTINE?

OLIVE YOU.

13 *More Tricky Questions*

These are just as tricky as the "tricky questions" on earlier pages. Don't look at the answers until you have tried your best to figure out the "catch" in each one.

THE TRAMP AND THE TRAIN

A tramp was walking down a railroad track when he saw a fast express train speeding toward him. Of course, he jumped off the track. But before he jumped, he ran ten feet *toward* the train. Why?

A HARD-BOILED PROBLEM

If it takes twenty minutes to hard-boil one goose egg, how long will it take to hard-boil four goose eggs?

HEAP TOUGH PROBLEM

A big fat Indian and a small thin Indian were sitting outside a teepee, each smoking a pipe. The little Indian was the son of the big Indian, but the big Indian was *not* the little Indian's father. How come?

14 Mr. Bushyhead's Problem

Mr. Bushyhead was driving through a strange town when he decided to stop, park his car, and get a haircut. He asked a boy where he could find a barbershop.

"We have only two barbers in this town," said the boy. "One of them has a shop at the north end of Main Street and the other has a shop at the south end."

Mr. Bushyhead walked north on Main Street until he reached one of the barbershops. It looked as if it hadn't been cleaned in months. Cut hair was all over the floor. The barber himself needed a shave and his haircut looked terrible.

Mr. Bushyhead walked in the other direction until he came to the second barbershop. It looked neat and cheerful inside. The floor had been swept. The barber was neatly dressed, freshly shaved, and had a neat haircut.

Why did Mr. Bushyhead walk back to the *first* barbershop to get his haircut?

15 *Sneaky Arithmetic*

These are easy number problems, but if you try to answer them too quickly you'll probably make mistakes. They're fun to spring on friends.

1. How much is 1 times 2 times 3 times 4 times 5 times 6 times 7 times 8 times 9 times 0?

2. Divide 20 by ½ and add 3. What is the result?

3. How much does a brick weigh if it weighs 5 pounds plus half its own weight?

4. A farmer had 17 sheep. All but 9 died. How many were left?

5. How much is twice one half of 987,654,321?

A sign painter was in such a hurry to finish his work that he made some careless mistakes when he painted these four signs. He painted one letter of each word wrong. See if you can change the incorrect letter in each word so that all four signs read properly.

17 The Undecidables

Does this widget (which looks like a tool, but isn't) have two prongs or three? There isn't any answer, because if you look at one end you see three prongs; but if you look at the other end you see one slot, so there seem to be only *two* prongs, one on each end of the slot! Psychologists call it an "undecidable figure." No matter how long you study it, you just can't decide how it is constructed.

The next page shows three more undecidables: a wooden frame with three holes into which the widget's prongs are inserted, three nutty nuts to fasten the prongs to the frame, and a crazy crate for carrying all these undecidables until you decide what to do with them!

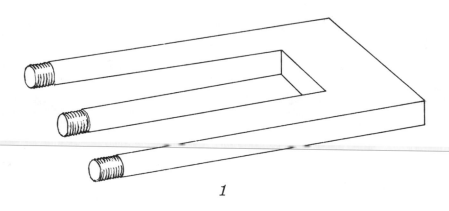

1

A three-pronged, one-slot widget.

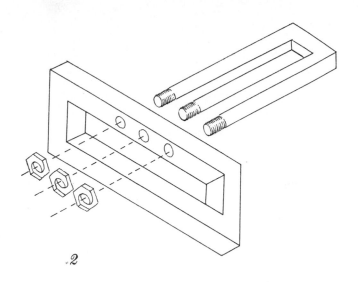

2

Frame for widget and nuts to hold it in place.

3

*Crazy crate for carrying widgets and
other undecidable objects.*

33

Last Sunday, when Sally went for a walk, she saw a policeman skipping rope; she saw a fire engine eating an ice-cream cone; she saw a squirrel humming a tune; she saw a puppy climbing a tree; she saw two robins playing hopscotch; she saw an organ grinder and his monkey.

Was Sally imagining all this? No, everything in the long sentence is right, except that it has been punctuated incorrectly. See if you can change the punctuation, without changing a single word, so that the sentence reads correctly.

THE MISPELLED WORD

Somewhere on this page there is a word that is not spelled correctly. Can you find it?

FLAPDOODLE'S WALK

Archibald Flapdoodle walked outside through a pouring rain for twenty minutes without getting a single hair on his head wet. He didn't wear a hat, carry an umbrella, or hold anything over his head. His clothes got soaked. How could this happen?

STAMPS TO STUMP YOU

It takes twelve one-cent stamps to make a dozen. How many four-cent stamps does it take to make a dozen?

WHAT DO YOU THINK?

There once was a race horse
That won great fame.
What-do-you-think
Was the horse's name.

A typitoon is a picture made by hitting typewriter keys. Here are a few examples. See if you can guess what they are. If there is a typewriter in your house, perhaps you can invent some new ones.

1   2

3   4

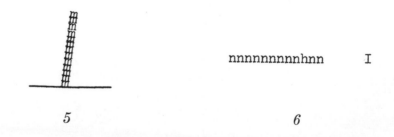

5   6

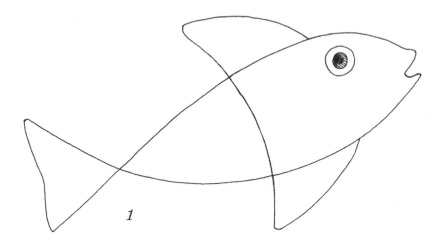

1

Get a pencil and a sheet of blank paper, then see if you can draw this fish in one continuous line without taking the pencil point off the paper, without going over any part of the line twice, and without crossing over any part of the line.

After you've learned how to draw the fish, see if you can draw the robot in the same way.

The eyes of the fish and robot are not part of either puzzle.

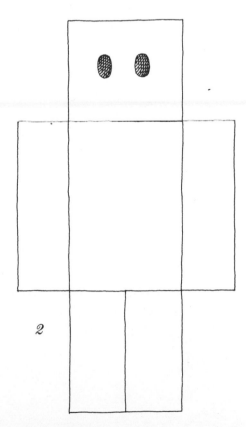

2

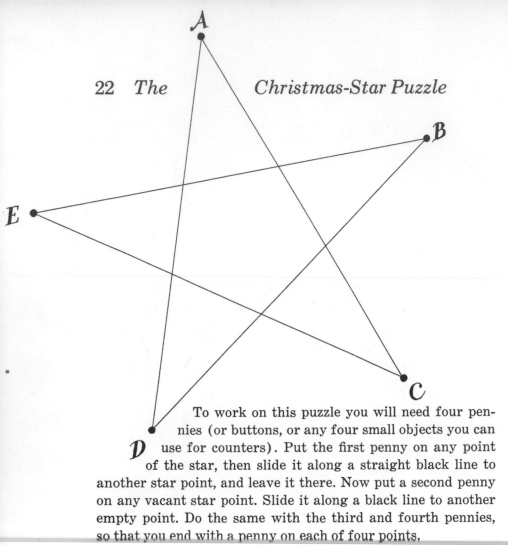

To work on this puzzle you will need four pennies (or buttons, or any four small objects you can use for counters). Put the first penny on any point of the star, then slide it along a straight black line to another star point, and leave it there. Now put a second penny on any vacant star point. Slide it along a black line to another empty point. Do the same with the third and fourth pennies, so that you end with a penny on each of four points.

It looks easy, but when you try it you are likely to find that there is no way to place the last penny. For example, suppose you:

1. Put a penny on A and slide it to C.
2. Put a penny on B and slide it to D.
3. Put a penny on B and slide it to E.

You can now place the last penny on A or B, but in either case, there is no empty point you can slide it to.

It *can* be done! And there is a secret that will enable you to do the puzzle for your friends, and do it so quickly that they will not be able to remember how you did it!

23 The Boring Bookworm

A ten-volume encyclopedia stands on the shelf as shown. Each volume is two inches thick. Suppose a bookworm starts at the front cover of Volume 1 and eats his way in a straight horizontal line through to the back cover of Volume 10. How far does the worm travel?

24 The Triangular Turkey

How many different triangles can you find in this picture of a Thanksgiving turkey?

25 Find the Best Words

The bull in this picture has just swallowed a time bomb that is set to go off in five minutes. Which of the four words below do you think best describes the situation?

Awful
Abominable
Dreadful
Shocking

Here is a picture of the same scene, after the bomb went off. Which word below is the best description of the picture?

Amazing
Silly
Messy
Noble

Zoo-lulus were created by Max Brandel for *Mad Magazine.**
What is a zoo-lulu? It is a printed name of an animal with
something added or done to it that makes you think of that ani-
mal. For example, you can stretch the *H* in *dac*|————|*shund*
so that the name *looks* like a dachshund! Or you can make the
first two *o*'s in *hòót owl* look like an owl's eyes.

Now see if you can guess the missing letters in *Mad*'s
eight zoo-lulus that are shown below and on the next page.

1. *GIRA? ? ?*

2. *SN? ? ?*

3. *PORC? ? ? ? ?*

4 SHA ? ?

5 C[stool] ?

6 RAB ? ?

7 TU ? ? ?

8 BA ?

27 Unscramble the Beast

The boy at the zoo started to call out the name of the animal he saw, but he became so excited that he got his words all mixed up. See if you can take all twelve of the letters in "Oh, it's a pom pup!" and rearrange them to make a single word that will be the name of the huge beast the boy is pointing to.

Have you ever added and subtracted letters instead of numbers?

For example, consider the following equation:

$$\text{1} \quad \text{🦴} - ONE + \text{👂} = \text{?}$$

The first picture is a picture of a bone, so we print the letters, B-O-N-E. We are told to subtract O-N-E from B-O-N-E, so we cross out O-N-E, which leaves only the B. Next, we must add E-A-R. When we do this, we get the word B-E-A-R. Bear is the animal that solves the equation!

Now see how good you are at this strange kind of arithmetic by working out the following equations. Each one gives the name of a familiar animal.

$$\text{2} \quad \text{👔} - E + \text{🐶} - \text{🎀} = \text{?}$$

3   $- Y + \bigcirc - M = \ ?$

4   $+ \ - \ = \ ?$

5   $- N + \ - \ + \ - \ = \ ?$

29 *The Undecidable Stairway*

Remember that three-pronged, one-slot widget on a previous page? Here's another undecidable figure: a crazy staircase.

If you walk around it clockwise, you can keep on going downstairs forever without ever getting any lower! And if you walk around it counterclockwise, you can keep on forever climbing up the stairs without getting any higher!

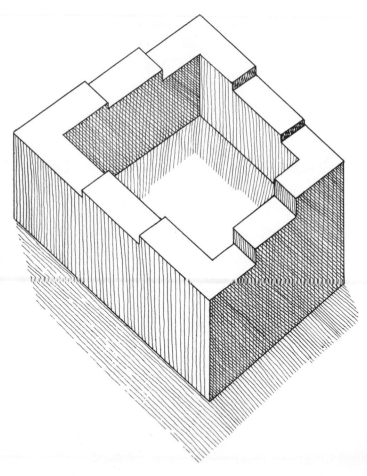

30 *More Sneaky Arithmetic*

1. A harmonica cost a dollar more than a pencil. Together they cost $1.10. How much did each cost?

2. A ribbon is 30 inches long. If you cut it with a pair of scissors into one-inch pieces, how many snips would it take?

3. Farmer Brown came to town with some watermelons. He sold half of them plus half a melon, and found that he had one whole melon left. How many melons did he take to town?

4. If you took 3 apples from a basket that contained 13 apples, how many apples would you have?

5. Nine thousand, nine hundred and nine dollars is written like this: $9,909. How fast can you write the figures for this sum of money: twelve thousand, twelve hundred and twelve dollars?

31   *How Clever are You?*

Are you good at thinking of simple ways to solve difficult problems that you sometimes come up against in everyday life? Suppose, for instance, that:

1. You see a truck that has become stuck beneath an underpass because it was an inch too tall to continue passing through. There is a filling station and garage a short distance down the road. The driver of the truck is starting to walk toward the garage to get help when suddenly a bright idea pops into your head. You tell the driver and five minutes later he is through the underpass and on his way.

What did you tell him to do?

2. You are a Boy Scout on a hike with your troop. After walking through a small town on your way to Mudville, you reach a spot where two roads cross. A signpost has been knocked over and is lying on its side. None of you knows which road leads to Mudville. Then you remember something that will solve your problem.

What do you remember?

3. You are playing a game of Ping-Pong in the back yard of a friend's house. When you miss the ball, it bounces across the lawn and rolls into a small but deep hole. The hole goes down too far for you to reach the ball with your hand, and the hole bends so much to one side that you can't get the ball by poking a stick into the hole. After a few minutes you think of an easy way to get the ball.

What did you think of ? ·

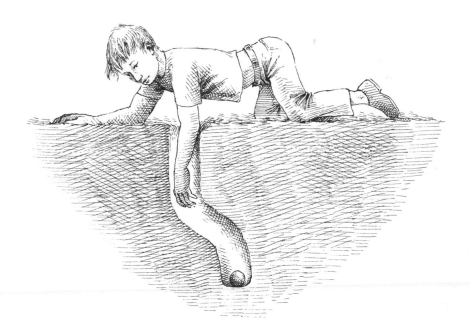

1. TURN GEORGE UPSIDE DOWN

Hold a dollar bill as shown in Figure 1, with Washington's face upright.

Fold down the top half (Figure 2).

Fold in half again, swinging right section back behind left one (Figure 3).

Fold in half again, swinging right section forward in front of left one (Figure 4).

Now unfold, swinging front section forward and to the right (Figure 5).

Unfold again, swinging front section forward and to the right (Figure 6).

Swing the front half forward and up (Figure 7).

If you have followed the illustrations exactly, Washington's face is now upside down! You seem to have unfolded the bill in the same way as you folded it. Why does the bill turn around?

1   WASHINGTON UPRIGHT

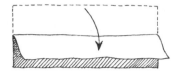

2   FOLD TOP DOWN

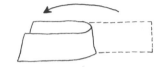

3   FOLD *BACK* AND TO THE LEFT

4   FOLD *FORWARD* AND TO THE LEFT

5   UNFOLD FROM FRONT

6   UNFOLD FROM FRONT

7   LIFT UP FRONT FLAP

8   WASHINGTON IS UPSIDE DOWN!

2. TURN GEORGE INTO A MUSHROOM

See if you can make two folds on a dollar bill to turn Washington into a mushroom.

3. FIND GEORGE'S KEY

Inspect the front of a dollar bill carefully. Can you find a picture of a door key?

4. THE POP-OFF CLIPS

Attach two paper clips to a folded dollar bill, exactly as shown in the picture. Hold the ends of the bill and pull the bill out flat. Can you guess what will happen to the clips? Try it and see.

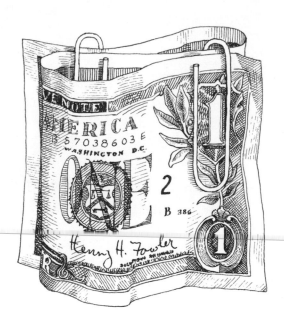

33 *Knock, Knock . . . Who's There?*

You've probably played "Knock, Knock" before, but just in case you haven't, it's a game that goes like this:

"Knock, knock," you say to a friend.

"Who's there?" he replies.

"Gorilla."

"Gorilla who?"

"*Gorilla* my dreams, I love you."

Your friend will laugh (you hope), if he gets the pun. And if he knows a good "knock-knock," *he'll* try it on you.

Before looking at the answers, see how many good "knock-knocks" you can invent for these five boys' names:

> 1. Hiawatha
> 2. Sam
> 3. Noah
> 4. Tarzan
> 5. Chester

And these five girls' names:

> 1. Carmen
> 2. Sharon
> 3. Celia
> 4. Sarah
> 5. Minnie

Mr. Kegler is trying to figure out how he can knock over one bowling pin at a time and always leave pins standing that will spell a word. He has just knocked down the second *T* and the remaining letters spell STARLING, which is the name of a bird. How can he bowl over a pin at a time and each time leave a familiar word, until only one pin that makes a word all by itself is left?

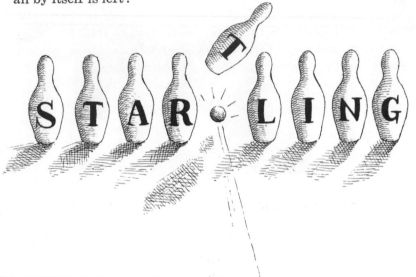

A lady had four pieces of gold chain. Each piece contained three links. She took the four pieces to a jeweler and asked him to join them together to make a bracelet, like this:

"I'll have to charge you a dollar for each link I cut apart and weld together again," the jeweler said. "Since I have to cut and weld four links, the job will cost you four dollars."

"Oh no it won't," said the lady (who was very good at puzzles). "It should cost only *three* dollars because you can make the bracelet by cutting and welding only *three* links."

The lady was right. Show how the job can be done in just the way she said.

MIDGE ON THE ELEVATOR

Midge lives on the twelfth floor of a modern elevator apartment building. Whenever she gets into the automatic elevator on the ground floor, and no one else is in the elevator, she pushes the button for floor 6, gets off on the sixth floor, and walks up the stairway to the twelfth floor. She would *much* prefer to ride the elevator all the way up to her floor. Why does she do this?

MRS. FUMBLEFINGER'S FUMBLE

Mrs. Fumblefinger was working in the kitchen when a loose ring, with a big diamond on it, slipped off her finger and fell smack into some coffee. Strange to say, the diamond did not get wet. Why?

THE SNEAKY WAITER

At Sloppy Joe's Restaurant a customer was shocked to find a fly in his coffee. He sent the waiter back for a fresh cup. After his first sip, the customer pounded on the table and shouted: "This is the *same* cup of coffee I had before!" How could he tell?

37 *A Pair of Eye Twiddlers*

TALL STILTS

Are the stilts that this clown is standing on bent in or out,
or are they straight?

TALL PROVERBS

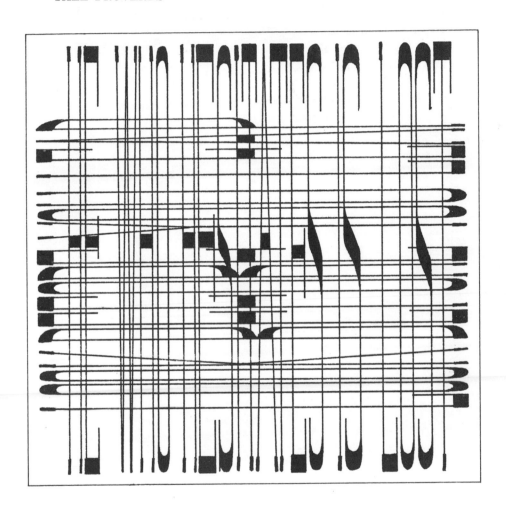

Can you read the two familiar proverbs printed above?

The owner of this barbershop likes puzzles and jokes, so he put up the sign that you see at the top of his window. When customers come in to ask him for a free shave and drink, he explains that the artist who made the sign for him forgot to add the proper punctuation.

See if you can add one exclamation mark and one question mark, each at the right spot in the sign, so that the sign expresses what the barber really wants to say to his customers.

Start at Mr. Mazo's necktie and find a way to reach the inside of his hat without crossing any lines. Use your finger or a toothpick, instead of a pencil, to follow the route, so you can show the puzzle to your friends without giving away the answer.

Old Mother Hubbard
Went to the cupboard
*   To get her poor dog a bone.*
When she got there,
The cupboard was bare,

and so Old Mother Hubbard cried out, "OICURMT!"

Can you figure out the meaning of that strange exclamation?

41 *Solve the Bird Equations*

The equations on these two pages work the same way as the animal equations on previous pages except that each gives the name of a familiar bird. See how many of them you can solve.

1

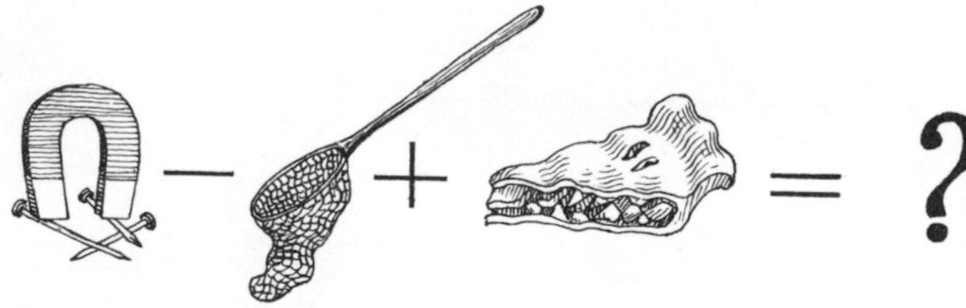

2

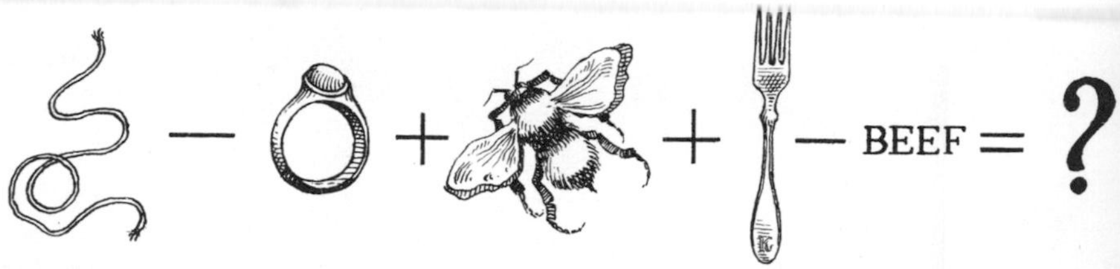

3   [image] — [image] + [image] = **?**

4 {
[image] + [image] — [image] +

[image] + **TON** — [image] = **?**
}

5   ☆ + [image] + [image] — [image] = **?**

THE KING AND THE ALCHEMIST

One day, centuries ago, an alchemist brought a small bottle to the king. "This bottle," said he, "holds a liquid so powerful that it will instantly dissolve anything it touches." How did the king know the man was lying?

BETSY AND PATSY

"We were born on the same day of the same year," said Betsy.

"And we have the same mother and father," said Patsy.

"But we're not twins," said Betsy.

Can you explain?

THE PURPLE PARROT

"I guarantee," said the salesman in the pet shop, "that this purple parrot will repeat every word it hears." A customer bought the bird, but found that the parrot wouldn't speak a single word. Nevertheless, what the salesman said was true. How could this be?

43   The Concealed Proverb

In each of the sentences below a word is concealed, such as the word "no" that is marked in the fifth sentence. If you can find the other buried words and read them in order, they will form a well-known proverb.

1. The word buried here has only one letter.

2. Did you find a jelly roll in Gaskin's Bakery?

3. It's the best one I've ever seen.

4. The rug at her stairway was made in India.

5. He's an old friend.

6. Amos sold his bicycle to a friend.

44 *The Dime-and-Nickel Switcheroo*

Put three pennies, a nickel, and a dime on top of their pictures. By sliding one coin at a time, into a neighboring empty cell, can you make the dime and nickel change places? You are allowed to move a coin left or right, up or down, but not diagonally.

It's easy to switch the dime and nickel if you keep sliding the coins long enough, so try to figure out how to switch them with the smallest number of moves. It can be done in fewer than twenty moves, but it takes more than twelve.

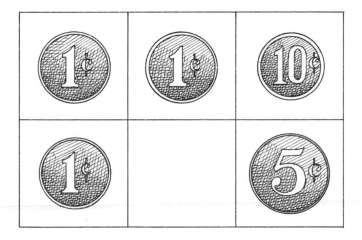

45 Mrs. Windbag's Gift

Professor Windbag likes to use big words and say everything in the most complicated way he can. When he handed a birthday present to his wife he said:

"My dear, here is a diminutive, aurum, truncated cone, convex on its summit and semiperforated with symmetrical indentations and a hollow interior."

Can you guess what is in the box?

CRAZY LINES

Which line is longest: the line from *A* to *B* or the line from *A* to *C?*

CRAZY CURVES

Are these curves circles or ovals?

47 *Shake Out the Cherry*

The matches in this picture represent a cocktail glass with a cherry inside. Put a paper match on top of each match in the picture.

Now see if you can pick up just two matches and place them so that the cocktail glass is upside down, and the cherry is *outside* the glass.

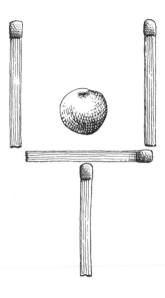

ANSWERS

1   *Ridiculous Riddles*

1. Super pickle. 2. A magnetized banana. 3. Here, kitty, kitty, kitty. 4. An embarrassed zebra. 5. Dwight D. Eiffel Tower. 6. With some root beer, two scoops of ice cream, and a hippopotamus. 7. *Very* carefully. 8. A lost camel. 9. A cherry that works at night as a grape. 10. It's the part of an apple you throw away. 11. A chair, a bed and a toothbrush. 12. A remote-control fig. 13. A baseball team with the measles. 14. Because they can't walk at all *hardly.* 15. Nothing. 16. A cow. 17. Tep on the brake, toopid! 18. He just ate a ranger.

2   *Handies*

1. Indian peeking over indoor television antenna. 2. Absent-minded professor scratching his head. 3. Midget playing the piano. 4. Help! I swallowed my toothbrush! 5. Tea (T) for two. 6. Turn hand upside down, with fingers in same position, and say: It's a dead *that.* 7. Helicopter looking for a place to land.

3   *Fun with Palindromes*

There are twelve palindromic words. Taken in order they are: radar, Hannah, I, redder, did, noon, wow, ma'am, Otto, a, pup, eye.

4   The Lost Star

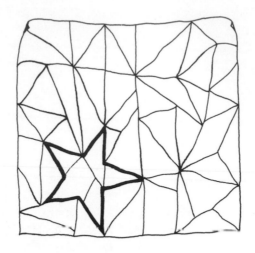

5   Find the Hidden Animals

1. Dog. 2. Gnu. 3. Monkey. 4. Beaver. 5. Bear. 6. Lion.
7. Camel 8. Cat.

6   Tricky Questions

HIGGS'S PIGS

None. Pigs can't talk.

PENNIES FOR SALE

One thousand, nine hundred and sixty-six pennies are worth $19.66, which is almost twenty dollars.

POP AND GRANDPOP

Yes. Strange as it may seem, Tom's father is forty and his grandfather, on his *mother's* side, is forty-six. The grandfather was twenty when Tom's mother was born and she was sixteen when Tom was born. Tom is now ten years old. (20 + 16 + 10 = 46.)

80

It's easy. First Jim crawls through the pipe in one direction. After he comes out, Tom crawls through it the other way.

7   *The Five Airy Creatures*

The little "creatures" are the five vowels: *A,E,I,O,U.* Jonathan Swift called them "airy" because they are actually made of air—the air that comes out of your throat and makes the vowel sounds.

8   *The Maze of the Minotaur*

The path to the Minotaur is shown by the dotted line.

START HERE

9 The Dime-and-Penny-Switcheroo

1. Slide the penny.
2. Jump the penny with the dime.
3. Slide the dime.
4. Jump the dime with the penny.
5. Jump the other dime with the other penny.
6. Slide the dime.
7. Jump the penny with the dime.
8. Slide the penny just jumped.

10 A Dozen Droodles for Nimble Noodles

1. Toothbrush with only two bristles.
2. A boy who needs a haircut.
3. The Wicked Witch of the West after Dorothy tossed a pail of water over her.
4. Four elephants sniffing a baseball.
5. Navel orange wearing a bikini.
6. Baby sleeping in dresser drawer.
7. Three little pigs on a foggy day.
8. A used lollipop.
9. Elephant scratching an ant's back.
10. Hard-fried egg turned upside down on a counter.
11. Man with bow tie that got caught in elevator doors.
12. Banana skipping rope.

11 Tantalizing Toothpick Teasers

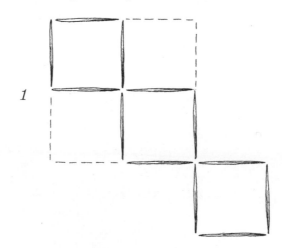

1

2

3 TEN

4

5

6

12 Read the Thriftigrams

1. I'm never as happy as I am when I'm with you. Love and kisses.
2. Have to take plane. Can you meet me at airport?
3. Will you be my Valentine? I love you.

13 More Tricky Questions

THE TRAMP AND THE TRAIN

The tramp had been walking along train tracks on a high, narrow bridge with no space on the sides where he could stand. When he saw the train speeding toward him, he was closer to the end of the bridge ahead of him than to the end behind him, so he ran toward the approaching train to get off the bridge as quickly as possible.

A HARD-BOILED PROBLEM

The same twenty minutes. You can put all the goose eggs in the same pan.

HEAP TOUGH PROBLEM

The big Indian was the little Indian's *mother*.

14 Mr. Bushyhead's Problem

The barber in the neat shop had the best haircut. Since there were only two barbers in town, his hair must have been cut by the *other* barber. Mr. Bushyhead decided to go to the barber who gave the best haircut.

15 Sneaky Arithmetic

1. If you noticed that zero at the end then you knew at once that the answer was zero, because zero times anything is zero.
2. 43. One half goes into 20 forty times, not ten.

84

3. 10 pounds. Two halves make a whole, so if the brick's total weight is the sum of 5 pounds and half the total weight, the other half must also be 5.
4. If all but 9 died, then of course 9 were left.
5. Twice one half of any number is that same number, so the answer is 987,654,321.

16   *The Careless Sign Painter*

The signs should read: QUIET, PUSH, EXIT, and WET PAINT.

18   *Sally's Silly Walk*

Last Sunday, when Sally went for a walk, she saw a policeman; skipping rope, she saw a fire engine; eating an ice cream cone, she saw a squirrel; humming a tune, she saw a puppy; climbing a tree, she saw two robins; playing hopscotch, she saw an organ grinder and his monkey.

19   *Still More Tricky Questions*

THE MISPELLED WORD

The word that is spelled incorrectly is the word "mispelled" in the problem's title. There should be another "s" in misspelled.

FLAPDOODLE'S WALK

Archibald was bald.

STAMPS TO STUMP YOU

Twelve. It takes twelve of anything to make a dozen. Even four-cent stamps.

The poem doesn't ask a question. The horse's name was *What-do-you-think*.

20 Guess The Typitoons

1. Boy watching baseball game through a hole in the fence. 2. Person watching a Ping-Pong game. 3. Row of soldiers (or cello players). 4. Row of bunnies (or bugs). 5. The leaning tower of Pisa. 6. Boy in third row raising his hand to ask teacher a question.

21 The Fish and the Robot

There are many ways to draw both figures according to the rules, but in every case you must always begin and end the single line at the spots marked with dots.

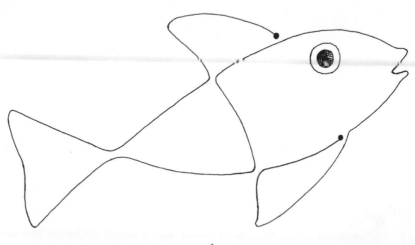

1

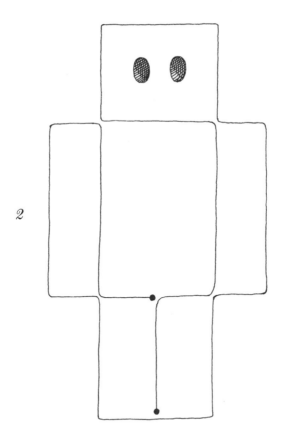

2

22 The Christmas-Star Puzzle

The secret: Put the first penny on any point you like and slide it to another point. After that, place each penny so you can slide it to the spot where the previous penny was *before* you slid it. For example:

1. Put a penny on A and slide it to C.
2. The previous penny was on A before you slid it, so put a penny on D and slide it to A.
3. The previous penny was on D before you slid it, so put a penny on B and slide it to D.
4. The previous penny was on B before you slid it, so put a penny on E and slide it to B.

23   The Boring Bookworm

The worm travels 16 inches. When a book stands on a shelf in front of you, its front cover is on the *right* side and its back cover is on the *left*. The worm travels, therefore, along the 16-inch path shown by the dotted line.

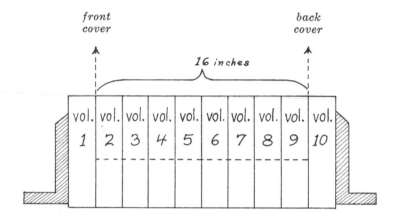

24   The Triangular Turkey

There are thirteen different triangles. No wonder it's an unlucky bird!

25   Find the Best Words

Abominable (a bomb in a bull) and *Noble* (no bull).

26   Zoo-lulus

Giraffe, snail, porcupine, shark, cow, rabbit, turkey, bat.

27   Unscramble the Beast

Hippopotamus.

28 Solve the Animal Equations

2. TIE − E + FINGER − FIN = TIGER
3. BABY − Y + MOON − M = BABOON
4. BADGE + PEAR − PEA = BADGER
5. CAN − N + MICE − ICE + ELBOW − BOW = CAMEL

30 More Sneaky Arithmetic

1. The harmonica cost $1.05, the pencil cost 5¢. Perhaps you thought the harmonica cost $1 and the pencil cost 10¢, but then the harmonica would cost 90¢ more than the pencil. To cost a dollar more, the harmonica must cost $1.05 and the pencil 5¢, because $1.05 minus 5¢ is $1.
2. Twenty-nine snips. The last two inches are divided by one snip.
3. Farmer Brown originally had 3 watermelons. He sold half of them (1½) plus half a melon, which is the same as saying that he sold 2 melons, leaving him with one whole melon as stated.
4. If you took 3 apples, you would *have* 3 apples!
5. $13,212. (12,000 + 1,200 + 12 = 13,212.)

31 How Clever are You?

1. You tell the driver to let some air out of his tires. This lowers the truck enough to let it through the underpass, then the driver can stop at the garage ahead and put the air back in his tires.
2. You remember the name of the town you have just left. If the signpost is replaced in the hole, with the name of the town you have left pointing back along the road you have just traveled, all the other signs will have to be pointing in the right direction.
3. Fill the hole with water from a hose and the Ping-Pong ball will float to the top.

1. TURN GEORGE UPSIDE DOWN

The secret is in the fold shown in the third picture. Note that it goes *back* instead of forward. When you undo this fold, however, as shown in the sixth picture, you undo it from the *front*. This is what turns the bill around. Practice until you can do the folds fast, without thinking, and you can have fun showing this to your friends. When *they* try it, the bill stays right side up!

2. TURN GEORGE INTO A MUSHROOM

3. FIND GEORGE'S KEY

The key is inside the round green seal at the right of Washington's picture.

4. THE POP-OFF CLIPS

The clips pop into the air and fall linked together!

33 *Knock, Knock. . . . Who's There?*

Boys' names: 1. *Hiawatha* high school dropout. 2. *Sam* enchanted evening. 3. *Noah* body knows the trouble I've seen. 4. *Tarzan* stripes forever. 5. *Chester* minute and I'll try to find out.

Girls' names: 1. *Carmen* get it! 2. *Sharon* share alike. 3. *Celia* later. 4. *Sarah* doctor in the house? 5. *Minnie* brave hearts are asleep in the deep.

Did you think of any better ones?

34 *Word Bowling*

STARTLING
STARLING
STARING
STRING
STING
SING
SIN
IN
I

35 *The Great Bracelet Mystery*

To make the bracelet without cutting more than three links, simply open all three links of one piece, then use those three links to join the other three links into a circle, like this:

36   And Still More Tricky Questions

MIDGE ON THE ELEVATOR

Midge is a small child and can reach up only as high as the sixth-floor button.

MRS. FUMBLEFINGER'S FUMBLE

The ring fell into a can of dry, ground coffee.

THE SNEAKY WAITER

The man had put sugar in his coffee before he found the fly in it. When he tasted the sugared coffee, he knew that the waiter had brought back the same cup of coffee.

37   A Pair of Eye Twiddlers

TALL PROVERBS

Hold the page flat in front of your nose and sight along it with one eye. (Be sure to keep the other eye closed.) You should be able to read the first proverb: *He who hesitates is lost.*

Now turn the book so you can sight along the page, the same way as before, but from the right side. You should be able to read the second proverb: *Look before you leap.*

The proverbs give opposite advice. Which do you think is the best to follow?

TALL STILTS

The stilts are perfectly straight! You can prove it by putting the edge of a ruler along them or by holding the page flat in front of one eye and looking at the stilts in the same way that you looked at the proverbs.

38   The Puzzling Barbershop Sign

WHAT! DO YOU THINK I'LL SHAVE YOU FOR NOTHING AND GIVE YOU A DRINK?

39 The Amazing Mr. Mazo

The dotted line shows how to go from Mr. Mazo's necktie to the inside of his hat.

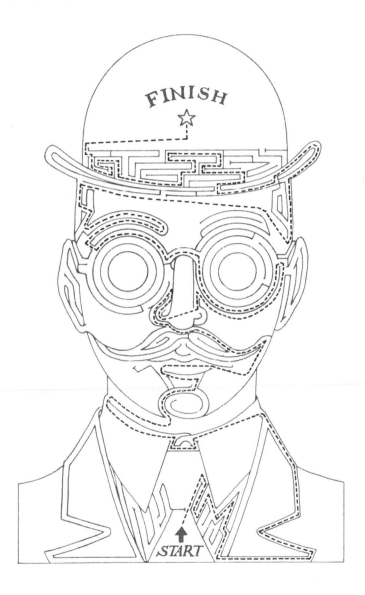

40 *Mother Hubbard's Cupboard*

Read the letters of Mother Hubbard's exclamation out loud and you will hear yourself saying "Oh, I see you are empty!"

41 *Solve the Bird Equations*

1. MAGNET – NET + PIE = MAGPIE
2. STRING – RING + BEE + FORK – BEEF = STORK
3. LACE – ACE + ARK = LARK
4. PIG + PANE – PAN + BEE + TON – BEET = PIGEON
5. STAR + TREE + SLING – TREES = STARLING

42 *The Last Tricky Questions*

THE KING AND THE ALCHEMIST

If the liquid dissolved anything it touched, it would dissolve the bottle.

BETSY AND PATSY

Betsy, Patsy, and a third sister were triplets.

THE PURPLE PARROT

The parrot was deaf.

43 *The Concealed Proverb*

The buried words form the proverb, "A rolling stone gathers no moss."

44 *The Dime-and-Nickel Switcheroo*

1. Nickel left
2. Dime down
3. Penny right
4. Nickel up
5. Penny right
6. Penny down
7. Nickel left
8. Penny left
9. Dime up
10. Penny right
11. Penny down
12. Nickel right
13. Penny up
14. Penny left
15. Penny left
16. Dime down
17. Nickel right

45 *Mrs. Windbag's Gift*

Mr. Windbag is saying that he is giving his wife a gold thimble.

46 *More Eye Twiddlers*

CRAZY LINES

The two lines are the same length, as you can prove by measuring them.

CRAZY CURVES

The curves are circles. You can prove this by measuring the distances from the central spot to different points on the same curve. You'll find that on any curve, all points along it are the same distance from the center.

47 *Shake Out the Cherry*

The two matches are moved like this:

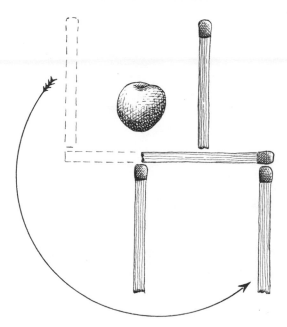